THE UNFORGETTABLE ELEPHANT

Laurie Platt Winfrey

Walker and Company • 720 Fifth Avenue • New York, New York 10019

First published in the United States of America in 1980 by the Walker Publishing Company, Inc.

Published simultaneously in Canada by Beaverbooks, Limited, Pickering, Ontario.

Cloth   ISBN: 0-8027-0650-9
Paper   ISBN: 0-8027-7157-2

Library of Congress Catalog Card Number: 79-91753

Designed by Joyce C. Weston
Printed in Japan
10 9 8 7 6 5 4 3 2 1

"Some elephants . . . have more understanding, and more discretion and intelligence than any kind of people I have met with."

Ludovico di Varthema
Itineria
Rome, 1510

There is no creature among al [sic] the Beasts of the world which hath so great and ample demonstration of the power and wisedome of almighty God as the elephant.

Edward Topsell
The Historie of Foure-Footed Beastes
London, 1658

CERTAIN ANIMALS HAVE a special charm for us humans because we see them as a funhouse mirror image of ourselves or our world. Monkeys and apes intrigue us—they are so like us! Lions may be beasts of superb feline grace and impressive power, but it is their lordly carriage and unruffled calm that leads us to call them kings. Pandas are the cuddly toys we had and loved as children.

Elephants, however, fascinate through attributes of size and strength that are solely their own, that are not human but superhuman. Watch a group of them setting up the Big Top on a city lot, carrying huge trees in an Indian forest, or simply *being*, in all their immensity, in a zoo. Slow moving, enormous—they captivate us.

Unique, too, is the elephant's physical form. The great bulky shape, finished off at one end with a sinuous (and practical) trunk, at the other with a tiny string of a seemingly useless tail, the whole set upon legs like tree stumps and punctuated by great flat flapping ears. Each time we see the beasts their huge grey bodies and anomalous appendages amaze us. What a caprice of God, or evolution, these creatures are!

The elephant's unique characteristics are the very stuff upon which to weave fancies, to place them in settings from the Garden of Eden to the realm of amiable King Babar. And it is our fancies that endow them with mystical power, with patience, good humor, and remarkable memory (as well as—charming contrast epitomizing the paradoxical—the deathly fear of mice).

Here are elephants—the most variegated herd ever assembled. Elephants that carry princes on their backs and an elephant who takes to the air for the delight of modern children; priceless elephants in silk and jade and ivory, curious elephants in wicker and wood, elephants that are buildings and bushes, symbolic elephants adorning banners and campaign buttons. Here are elephants carved in crystal-clear glass and elephants whose dull grey wrinkled hides have been overlaid with brilliant color; elephants who battle one another or fight man's wars for him—and even a suit of elephant armor.

They appear through the centuries—in religion, in art, in the crafts and lore of people around the world, in commerce and politics and humor. In every manifestation, the elephant remains one of the most enchanting of the world's beasts.

SINCE THE EARLIEST conception of the Garden of Eden, the elephant has been a part of the artist's imagination. Although Hieronymus Bosch is a painter known more for his tortured demons of the apocalypse, his representation of the elephant in his *Garden of Earthly Delights* (*opposite*) is more a study from nature. Perhaps he found no need to embellish as fantastic a creature as he might possibly imagine. In Theodore de Bry's engraving of another biblical scene (*below*), "the animals file two by two . . .," led by the elephants past a thankful Noah.

THE EARLIEST EVIDENCE of the domestication of the elephant are the seals unearthed at Mohenjo-Daro in India which date from 1500 B.C. and show the elephant fitted with a cloth blanket (*opposite, above*). By the fifth century B.C. the Etruscans had incorporated the working elephant into their art (*below*) and their domestic lives.

Animal scenes were popular throughout the classical world; one of their themes was the inclusion of as many different creatures as possible. In the fourth-century Roman mosaic (*opposite, below*) the animals and birds are drawn together by the music of a harp.

LOOKING IN SILHOUETTE LIKE a running elephant, this fantastic creature is made up of acrobatic dancing girls (*below*). The seventeenth-century author J.B. Tavernier describes it in his *Travels*: "These women have so much suppleness that when the king wished to visit . . ., nine of them very cleverly represented the form of an elephant, four making the four feet, four others the body, and one the trunk, and the king mounted above . . . in that way made his entry into the town."

Whether a delightful genre scene or a visualization of Thai divinities (*opposite*), the composite elephant is a feat of imaginative draftsmanship.

"Who is to blame the naturalists," a scholar asks, "for their hesitation in identifying the unicorn and dragon as mythological when in a single century living examples of the elephant, giraffe, and rhinoceros had presented themselves for all to see and wonder about?"

Here elephants monopolize an accordion-style picture book from Thailand's Ayudhia Period, in the seventeenth or early eighteenth century.

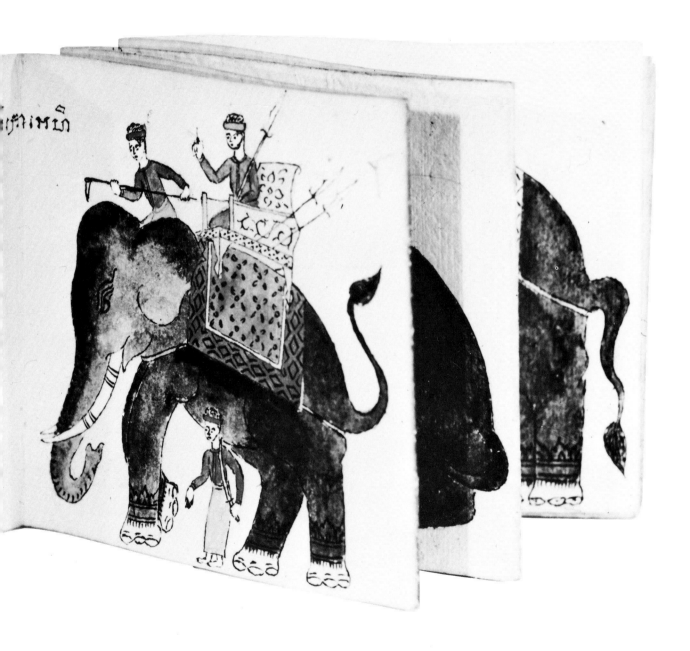

THOUGH THE CULT of the white elephant was central to Thai mythology, a certain freewheeling speculation about other kinds of elephants is evidenced in these watercolors from a nineteenth-century manuscript. There was a superstition that an elephant with a spotted trunk would bring death to the king—what disasters the possession of the elephant below might bring can only be imagined. Whimsically, the artist offers an enchantment of orange and green and pale blue elephants (*opposite, above*) but turns realistic enough to observe correctly that the elephant cannot stomach crabs (*below, bottom*).

The artistic license of the paintings is evoked again in the contemporary porcelain stand (*opposite, below*).

IN CHINA, elephants, a symbol of strength, were commonly represented in the designs of ritual bronzes that were then buried with their owners. These two wine vessels are from the earliest Chinese dynasties, the Shang, ca. 1500 B.C. (*below, right*), and the Chou, from the tenth century B.C. (*opposite*). The bronzes were used for preparing food as an offering to the most revered of all Chinese divinities, their ancestors. Jade was prized in China for its luminous warmth and was normally reserved for lofty subjects, unlike the small figure of the youth with his elephant from the T'ang Dynasty (*below, left*).

INDRA, THE HINDU god of the heavens, was pictured riding on a mighty white elephant known as Airavata, believed to be the first elephant in the world (*below, right*). The six-tusked elephant god also appears in the Buddhist ritual as the vehicle upon which the attendant to Buddha sat (*opposite*). Buddhists cast the white elephant in the role filled by the dove in Christianity. "The future Buddha, who had become a superb white elephant, descended thence, and approached [his mother, Maya]. Holding in his silvery trunk a white lotus flower, and uttering a far-reaching cry, he entered the golden mansion, and thrice doing obeisance to his mother's couch, he gently struck her right side, and seemed to enter her womb" (*below, left*).

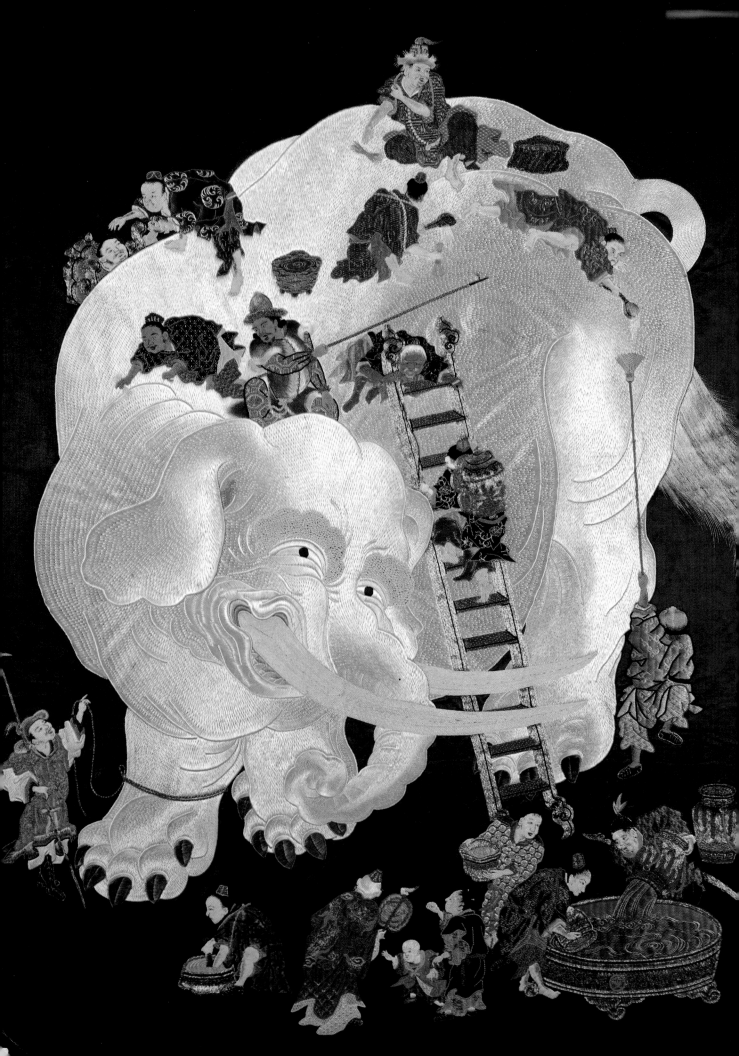

THE WHITE ELEPHANT enjoyed a cult that accorded it all the privileges of a living god. Particularly in Thailand, the white elephant was so sacred that not even the king was allowed upon its back, and its possession could occasion wars. "The king of Pegu [Burma], hearing that the king of Siam had two white elephants, sent messengers to him to buy them offering any sum . . . The king of Siam refused . . . [which] so enraged the king of Pegu . . . that he sent an army . . . and took not only his two elephants, but his whole country."

Anna Leonowens, the English governess at the Siamese court in 1870, recorded a speech welcoming a new white elephant. "Most Royal Elephant! We beg that you will not think too much of your father and mother . . . [or] regret leaving your native forests, because there are evil spirits there . . . and wild beasts that howl. And that is not all, in the forest you have no servants, and it is very unpleasant to sleep with dust and filth adhering to your body . . ."

Caring for the sacred elephant has never been more beautifully expressed than in the eighteenth-century Japanese silk embroidery (*opposite*). The behemoth balances eight diligent scrubbers and a full bucket of water on his back. It was so expensive to keep a white elephant in its necessary station with its own servants, palaces, musicians, and jewelry that one sly prince gave one to a feudal rival, thus guaranteeing financial ruin and passing the term "white elephant" on to those properties that cost more to maintain than the owner can manage.

GUARDIAN ELEPHANTS were erected at most Indian temples and sacred places. Their presence was meant to inspire the worshipful to elevate their thoughts to an attitude proper to religious observance. The statues (*opposite, below*) guard the entrance of the Nemnath temple at Mt. Abu. The eighth-century relief (*below*) shows the crowd of faithful and royal elephants at the auspicious moment when the River Ganges first flowed upon the earth.

Maharajas enlisted elephants as palace guardians not only as an act of homage to the gods but as an impressive sign of earthly good fortune (*opposite, above*).

INDIAN PAINTING reached its highest achievement under the great Mogul king Akbar in the sixteenth century. The finest examples of the Mogul school are not only lively and realistic but contain elements of individual portraiture. The miniature (*opposite*) is from the *Akbar-nama*, or History of Akbar, and depicts the king and his courtiers crossing the river Jumna on richly caparisoned elephants.

A pair of elephants serve as formidable sentries on an ivory comb (*below*).

"The procession was grand beyond conception; it consisted of about twelve hundred elephants, richly caparisoned, drawn up in a regular line, like a regiment of soldiers. About one hundred elephants in the centre had howdahs, or castles covered with silver; in the midst of these appeared the nabob, mounted on an uncommonly large elephant, within a howdah covered with gold, richly set with precious stones." This eyewitness account of the wedding of a high Indian official in 1795 is reflected in the miniature (*opposite*) from the *Shah-nameh*.

The superbly decorated state elephants of H.H. the Maharaja of Gwalior (*below, left*) stand in an off-duty moment before the start of the 1903 durbar, or elephant procession, in Delhi (*below, right*).

GANESHA, the Hindu god of wisdom, good fortune, and prudence and the "remover of obstacles" is one of the best loved deities in India. He is represented with the head of an elephant and the body of a man, carrying a bowl of sweets from which, judging by his belly, he indulges freely. Learned and amiable looking, his image appears over the doors of Indian shops and banks, in temple carvings such as at Kajurajo (*below right*), in sculpture (*below, left*), and in popular versions like the papier mâché mask opposite.

AN ANCIENT METHOD of hunting elephants was to prepare a pit furnished with a sharp stake (*below, right*). Pliny reports in his *Natural History*, "In Africa they take them in pitfalls; but as soon as an elephant gets into one, the others . . . immediately collect boughs of trees and pile up heaps of earth, and then endeavor with all their might to drag it out."

When hunting elephants for training, the Indian method was more humane. Either tame ones, called *koonkies*, were set out as bait to lure the wild, or an entire herd was driven into an enclosure (*below, left*). After two months of training, the keeper, or *mahout*, was ready to unchain his large pupil and test the effects of his tutelage (*opposite*).

A.B.C. Der Hottentotten Manier die Elephanten zu fangen.

TIGER HUNTS were a special passion of the Moguls, for whom personal bravery was a point of honor. In the painting (*overleaf*), armed horsemen encircle the tiger while Akbar and his son Jahangir prepare for the kill. Jahangir was a man of excesses and at one time possessed twelve thousand elephants, four thousand dogs, and maintained a harem of five thousand women and one thousand young men.

THOUGH WILD ELEPHANTS occasionally fight, theirs is more of a sparring to establish a loose hierarchy and to avoid unnecessary conflict. Once captured, the elephant would leave his peaceable kingdom and learn to fight in his master's wars and against his fellow elephants. Only a king could order an elephant fight. Unlike the elephants who lived to fight another day, their riders thought themselves fortunate if they lost only a limb. The combat would be considered finished when one elephant brought the other to the ground.

EMPERORS AND KINGS have found the fully armed war elephant a creature worth having in their armies. Equipped with a manned fortresslike howdah spitting fire, arrows, and slinging stones, the elephant below is capable of holding his own against a bewildering force of armed bulls, lions, and bears.

The Roman Emperor Galerius's use of elephants to defeat the Persians in 296 A.D. is commemorated in the relief (*opposite*) from Salonique, and Alexander the Great's victory over Porus, king of the Punjab, on the coin (*opposite, left*). Perhaps the most renowned example of elephant war strategy was Hannibal's crossing of the Alps in 218 B.C. Trekking his Carthaginian army and his thirty-seven elephants over the mountains, he was able to outflank his Roman enemy and lay siege to Italy. He was a brilliant military commander who today is remembered only for his daring with elephants (*opposite, right*).

IN ASIA THE WAR elephant was the dominant animal on the field of battle, important as much for its psychological impact as for its effectiveness as a military machine. A ring of heavily armored and war-painted elephants (*opposite*), all stamping and trumpeting and rumbling inexorably inward toward the battling in the center, had a total impact not only on the soldiers but on the horses, which become terrified in the presence of the huge beasts.

Elephants were the ancient equivalent of the armored tank in Asian warfare. The astonishing piece of elephant armor (*below*) was a trophy won by Lord Clive at the battle of Plassey in 1757. He brought it back to England where it now dominates the armories at the Tower of London.

WHEN IN "MUSTH," a condition that occurs somewhat periodically in male elephants, the animal's temporal glands, located near his eyes, become swollen with an oily discharge, signaling a period of ill humor and unpredictable behavior. In extreme cases the male's temper can be so aroused and maddened as to put him in the category of the rogue, destroying crops, wrecking villages, turning on his trainer.

The only recourse then is to destroy him, as shown in this second-century Indian relief (*below, right*) of the subjugation of the mad elephant Nalagiri.

While musth is primarily an Asiatic trait, the African species has never been domesticated as successfully and is by its nature capable of dangerous behavior (*opposite*).

AFRICAN TRIBAL DANCES often center on the elephant as a symbol of masculine prowess. The M'waash, a M'boy mask (*below, left*) is made from leather, cowrie shell beads, and raffia. A tassled version appears on a Kuba dancer in Mushenge, Zaïre (*below, right*). African masks are striking and forceful in their abrupt forms. The helmet mask (*opposite*) representing an elephant was made by the Ogoni in Nigeria.

SUCCESS IN HUNTING was a universal need, and representations of the elephant appear in the earliest African art that survives. An ancient example is the fragment of an elephant head from Nigeria. The wood mask with geometric design (*opposite*) is from the Ivory Coast.

THE ASHANTI OF GHANA are a great tribe who once monarchically ruled the Gold Coast and controlled the gold mines. The gold wire elephants (*below*) evolved from the brass animal weights used for measuring gold dust.

The leopard was fierce and beautiful and represented royal power; the elephant, bulky and strong, represented the lesser chieftains. A subchief of the Ebrie on the Ivory Coast poses with his elephant staff.

A house painting in Abidjan and a rattan rug from Nairobi attest to the variety of the African interpretation of one animal.

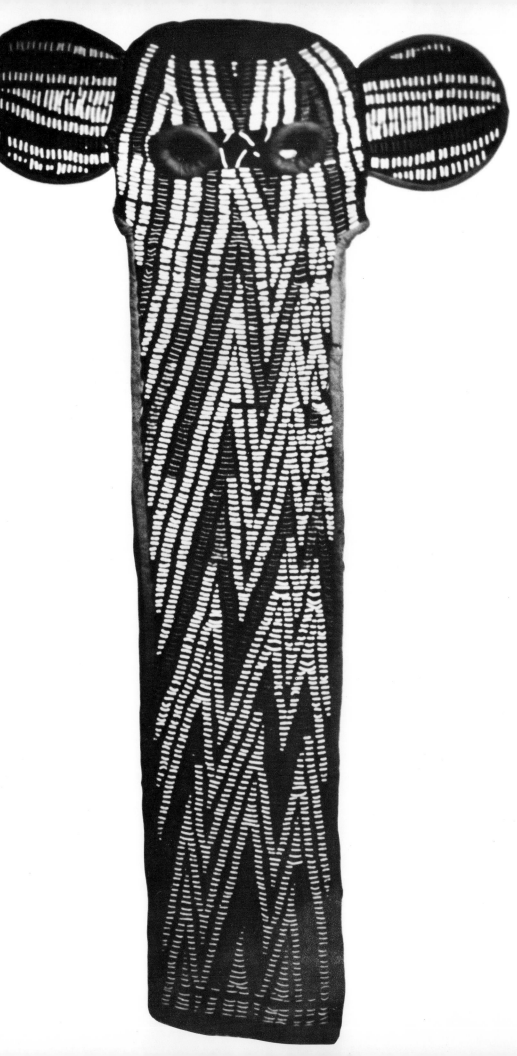

To each tribe or group of tribes, masks have a special significance, not only in the legends they record but also in their power and function within the society. The grasslands was the home of most of the art-producing tribes in the Cameroons, and the style is the most homogeneous of any large region in Africa. The two elephant masks shown here are boldly conceived and forcefully executed.

Raco maior cunctoꝝ serpentiū siue am
mantium omniū sup̃ terrã. hunc gre
ci draconta uocant. unde & deriuatū
est in latinum. ut draco dicerē̃. Qui sepe
ab speluncis abstractus ferꝰ in aerem. conci
tatur̃ꝗ ppℓ eum aer. Est autē cristatꝰ. oꝛe
paruo. & artis fistulis p quas trahit spm̃.
& linguam exerat. Vim autē non in dentib;

TO THE TWELFTH-CENTURY artist who had never seen an elephant, the sum of its legendary parts often resulted in a quite extraordinary whole. Superstitions regarding elephants grew up alongside the myths, so that an elephant could be thought capable of surviving mortal combat with a serpent (*opposite*) while being afraid of mice.

The Arab artist (*below, left*) has given his elephant booties and a chain-link trunk, but has obviously seen the subject at first hand, unlike the illuminator below, whose elephant with the ears of a bear, the eyes of a damsel, cloven hooves, and an unmuscled trunk cause the griffen to gape and the man's hair to stand on end.

An elephant, natures great
   master-peece,
the only harmlesse great
   thing; the giant
of beasts; who thought, no
   more had gone, to make
   one wise
(yet nature hath given him
   no knees to bend)
himselfe he up-props, on
   himselfe relies,
and foe to none, suspects no
   enemies,
still sleeping stood; vex't not
   his fantasie
Blacke dreames; liken an
   unbent bow, carelesly
   His sinewy Proboscis did
   remisly lie.

John Donne
The Progress of the Soul

The elephant hath joints, but
   none for courtesy:
his legs are legs for
   necessity, not for flexure.

William Shakespeare
Troilus and Cressida

THE APPEARANCE of an elephant was so astonishing to the people of the Middle Ages that when one was brought to England, the whole of London flocked to see it and Matthew Paris drew it twice, describing it "a show piece of unheard-of novelty" in his 1255 London chronicle.

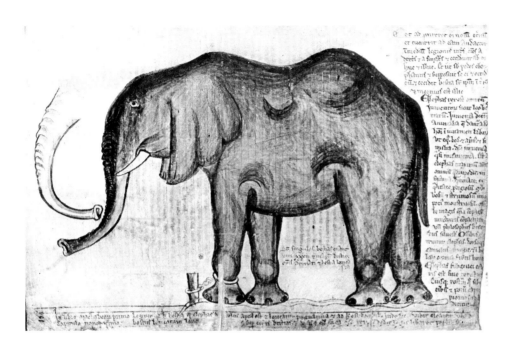

So geographers, in Afric maps,
With savage pictures fill their gaps,
and o'er unhabitable downs place elephants for want of towns.

Jonathan Swift
On Poetry, A Rhapsody

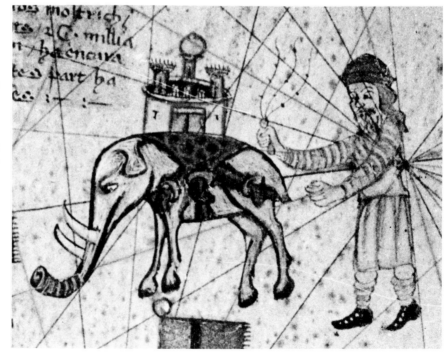

WHAT INTERESTED REMBRANDT, Tiepolo, and Goya in their elephant studies was the character of the creature. The elephant of G. B. Tiepolo (*opposite, above*), a century after Rembrandt, still was anatomically unsound but managed nevertheless to convey a careful intelligence. And Goya in his etching (*opposite, below*) has given his beast a tense watchfulness and vulnerability. But it is Rembrandt, with a few masterful strokes of his pencil (*below*), who has managed to capture with astonishing conviction the wrinkled folds of the skin, the enormous weight of the body, and the great character in the massive head.

PLANT SCULPTURE has been traced as far back as the ancient Egyptians and Romans. Topiary can take any form, from geometric spheres and pyramids to clipper ships and animals. Ornamental topiary was a part of the formal English garden and made its appearance in America on southern plantations and at the northern estates of wealthy landowners. A living sculpture can require as many as twenty years of painstaking trimming, shaping, and coaxing to reach maturity, only to have a frost or storm eat away a vital appendage overnight.

DESIGNED IN CRYSTAL by the American
sculptor Bruce Moore, the elephants
(*opposite*) stride along, trunks aloft, great
ears flapping, while egrets feed on
the insects stirred up by their heavy steps.

Less detailed and majestic than the
single trumpeters, the herd (*below*),
seemingly all trunks, browses among
imaginary acacia trees.

FOR CENTURIES, IVORY and slaves were Africa's two main exports. The insatiable demand for ivory has resulted in the near extinction of the African elephant, and this crisis is unexpectedly illustrated by the Chinese artist who carved the sculpture below (*bottom*). Ostensibly a community bathing scene, carved from a single tusk, the elephants actually appear to have been startled by a hidden danger into a stampede for their lives—an ironic tribute to the beast who died for this carving.

Ivory is an ideal material for carving and throughout history has been used for sculpture, as in the twelfth-century altar support from Orissa (*opposite, below*) and for ornamentation (*opposite, above*). The nineteenth-century ivory chess set (*below, top*) depicts the British raj in India.

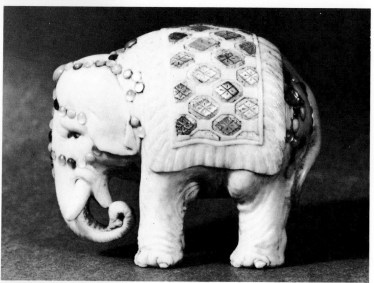

BEFORE THE JAPANESE adopted pocketed western garb, the well-dressed gentleman carried a small purse that was secured to his kimono sash with a *netsuke*, or toggle. These ornaments, finely worked in ivory, lacquer, glass, and wood, might represent birds, aquatic creatures, the erotic interests in Japanese life, legends, literary and religious subjects, or animals like the elephants shown here from the Raymond Bushell Collection.

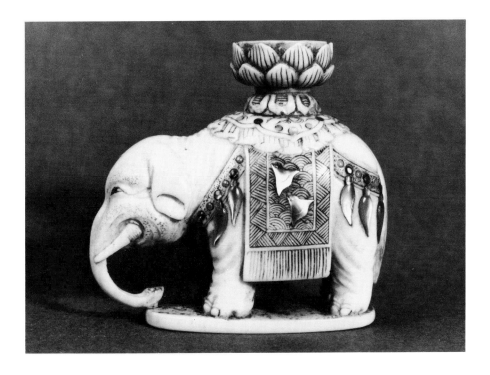

WHEN IT COMES to an animal shaped like the elephant, the silversmith's imagination could be limitless. The elephant might resemble an African wild boar or could find itself as diminutive as a mouse compared to its surrounding rock crystal cave. It might triumphantly bear an inch-wide salt bowl, or, when cast in the weight of solid silver, achieve a true representation of its massive self.

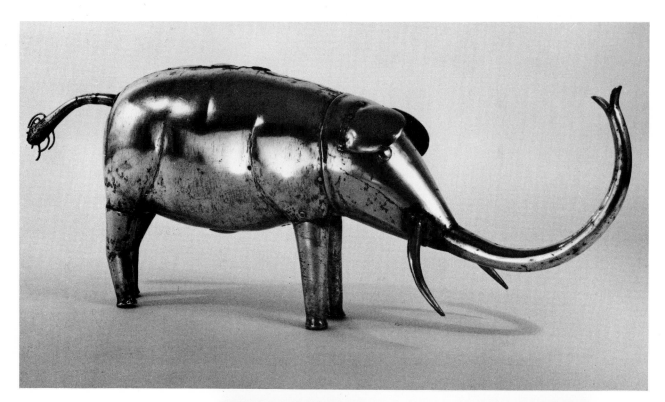

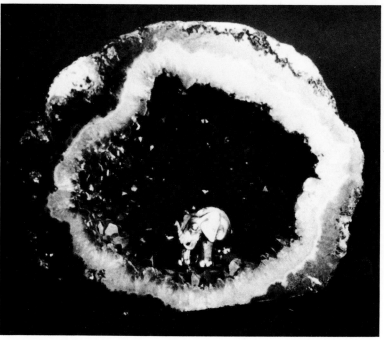

THE ENTERTAINMENT at the earliest recorded circuses in Rome pitted wild animals against each other and against men, more in the tradition of the modern bullfight than today's circus. As late as the sixteenth century, elephant entertainment continued to be patterned after war games, as shown by Antoine Caron's gently titled *Carousel de l'éléphant* (*below*). However, by 1796 when the first elephant came to America (*bottom*), he was billed as "the most respectable animal in the world . . . [though] some days he has drank [sic] 30 bottles of porter, drawing the corks with his trunk."

If this were not feat enough, by 1899 the Ringling Brothers elephants had formed a brass band with the dubious boast of being louder than a thousand human bandsmen (*opposite*).

VAN AMBURGH & CO. S. MAMMOTH MENAGERIE.

THE BABY ELEPHANT JENNY LIND.

THE SMALLEST LIVING ELEPHANT EVER EXHIBITED IN AMERICA

FROM THE LARGEST to The Smallest to The Cutest, the language of The Greatest Show on Earth deals in superlatives. Van Amburgh's "mammoth menagerie" included the baby elephant, Jenny Lind (*opposite, above*), "the smallest living elephant ever exhibited in America." Unlike her namesake, the popular Swedish soprano, she was accompanied everywhere by a chaperone.

HACHALIAH BAILEY bought his first elephant in 1808, eleven years after her arrival in the new country. Old Bet and Hach Bailey (pictured *below*) started the farmers and drovers of Somers, New York, on a new venture of social and economic importance with his "educational shows." In 1827 Bailey erected a wooden likeness of Old Bet on a granite shaft in front of his aptly named hotel, where she stands today. Although the circus people left Somers for Virginia in the 1830s, the circus spirit remains central to the town's pride, as shown in the quilt (*below, right*) made for the Bicentennial.

P.T. BARNUM'S GREATEST SHOW ON EARTH & THE GREAT LONDON CIRCUS COMBINED WITH

JUMBO THE PRIDE OF THE BRITISH HEART, HER MAJESTY, THE QUEEN, HER CHILDREN AND GRAND CHILDREN. & OVER ONE MILLION & A QUARTER OF ENGLISH CHILDREN HAVE RIDDEN ON HIS BROAD BACK IN SEVENTEEN YEARS.

SANGER'S ROYAL BRITISH MENAGERIE & GRAND INTERNATIONAL ALLIED SHOWS.

JUMBO, for seventeen years the Pride of the British Heart, was bought by the American showman P. T. Barnum in 1881, and as one writer commented, the reaction of dismay and horror in England could only have been exceeded by the sale to the Americans of Queen Victoria herself. By then Jumbo no longer displayed the amiability that had allowed over a million English children, royal and otherwise, to ride on his back (*opposite, above*).

Although Jumbo was a dignified twenty-two years old when he left for America, he inspired this bubble-blowing toy that portrays him as positively infantile. He delighted the North Americans for only three years before he was tragically killed by a train while leaving the circus grounds in Ontario.

Echelle de   5   10   15. Toises

Profil de l'Edifice sur la longueur.

AFTER THE EXTRAVAGANT TASTES of the royal court at Versailles, the French had little trouble accommodating themselves to the notion of a folly—an elephant palace in the center of Paris. Proposed by Charles François Ribart in 1758 to honor Louis XV, this "Grand Kiosque" represented the apogee of the elephant motif in art and architecture in western Europe. The exterior plan (*below, left*) was astonishing in itself, with a statue of the king astride the tower overlooking the trunk that cascaded water down upon admiring mermaids. The interior (*opposite*) included not only kitchens, offices, a grand staircase (*below, right*), and baths but a reception hall in the hind quarters fashioned to resemble a glen with its own running brook, and a theater in the front. The king's throne was placed in the head. Had these plans materialized we might now consider the storming of the elephant of Paris as we consider the storming of the Bastille in French history.

THE UNITED STATES had its own fad for elephant architecture in the late nineteenth century, most notably embodied in Lucy, the Margate Elephant, in Atlantic City (*opposite, above*). Lucy was built by a real estate developer in 1881 as an attraction for prospective buyers. Her howdah in place, she stands six stories high, is sculpted of nearly a million pieces of wood beneath her tin skin, and weighs ninety tons.

By 1970 Lucy was showing the ravages of the years and exposure to the salt air. She had gaping wounds in her sides, a bandaged trunk, and an ill-conceived howdah replacing the original, which was lost to a storm in the 1920s (*below*). Facing imminent demolition, Lucy was rescued by a group of volunteer citizens who formed the "Save Lucy Committee" and lobbied successfully for her designation as a National Historic Landmark (*opposite, below*). Not so fortunate was the fate of Lucy's twin at Coney Island (*below, right*) who was destroyed by fire in 1908.

ANIMALS PLAYING THE HUMAN FOOL in human garb made an instant success of caricaturist Jean Grandville when his *Metamorphoses du Jour* appeared in 1828. His mimicry of the fashions of his time heightened each animal's natural shape, as did his rendering of political personalities through familiar animals that are surprising in a new context. Increasingly politicized and anti-Royalist, Grandville added to his prodigious success with his portrayal of the Duke of Chartres as the great horned owl.

LXVIII.

La promenade.

XXVII.

La mienne est assurée aussi, j' m'en moque.

"THIS is the Elephant's Child having his nose pulled by the Crocodile. He is much surprised and astonished and hurt, and he is talking through his nose and saying, 'Led go! You are hurtig be!' He is pulling very hard, and so is the Crocodile; but the Bi-Coloured-Python-Rock-Snake is hurrying through the water to help the Elephant's Child. All that black stuff is the banks of the great grey-green, greasy Limpopo River (but I am not allowed to paint these pictures), and the bottly-tree with the twisty roots and the eight leaves is one of the fever trees that grow there."

"THIS is just a picture of the Elephant's Child going to pull bananas off a banana-tree after he had got his fine new long trunk. I don't think it is a very nice picture; but I couldn't make it any better, because elephants and bananas are hard to draw. The streaky things behind the Elephant's Child mean squoggy marshy country somewhere in Africa. The Elephant's Child made most of his mud-cakes out of the mud that he found there. I think it would look better if you painted the banana-tree green and the Elephant's Child red."

RUDYARD KIPLING gave the children of the early twentieth century the answers to many of their basic questions in his *Just So Stories:* how the leopard got his spots, how the camel got his hump—and how the elephant got his trunk (*opposite*).

Twenty-five years later, Walt Disney collaborated with Leopold Stokowski in a brilliant collection of animated musical pieces called *Fantasia.* A still from the film shows the "Dance of the Hours" put to music by Ponchielli. In 1941 Disney created the animated Dumbo, the lovable flying elephant, here conversing with Timothy the Mouse.

A Célesteville
les éléphants travaillent le matin
et l'après-midi ils font ce qu'ils veulent.
Ils jouent, se promènent, lisent, rêvent ...
Babar et Céleste
aiment faire une partie de tennis
avec Pilophage et Madame Pilophage.

BABAR, one of the best loved of all children's stories, was created by Jean De Brunhoff in 1931. Unlike Jean Grandville, who used animals to satirize the human condition, De Brunhoff made Babar a felicitous combination of the best qualities of man and elephant. Orphaned as an infant, Babar ran away to Paris, where he was befriended by "la vieille dame." Finally homesick for the jungle, he returned to marry Celeste and become the benevolent ruler of Celesteville. Over the years, Babar's family grew and his adventures continued from generation to generation, in the same way that the characters created by the father, Jean, are now guided by De Brunhoff's son Laurent.

Maintenant
Babar habite chez la vieille dame.
Le matin, avec elle,
il fait de la gymnastique,
puis il prend
son bain.

Babar va dîner
chez son amie la vieille dame.
Elle le trouve très chic
dans son costume neuf.
Après le dîner, fatigué,
il s'endort vite.

MARIANNE MOORE wrote of "the elephants, with their fog-colored skin and strictly practical appendages." These appendages have been put to strictly practical use indeed. The British in India made the best of both worlds in seeing the correlation between the elephant's trunk and the spout of a teapot they'd left at home, as in this Staffordshire piece from the eighteenth century (*below, left*). The elephant tests the wind in the iron weather vane (*opposite*) and amiably offers his trunk as a towel rack (*below, right*).

84

THE THIRD-TERM PANIC.

"An Ass, having put on the Lion's skin, roamed about in the Forest, and amused himself by frightening all the foolish Animals he met with in his wanderings."—SHAKSPEARE or BACON.

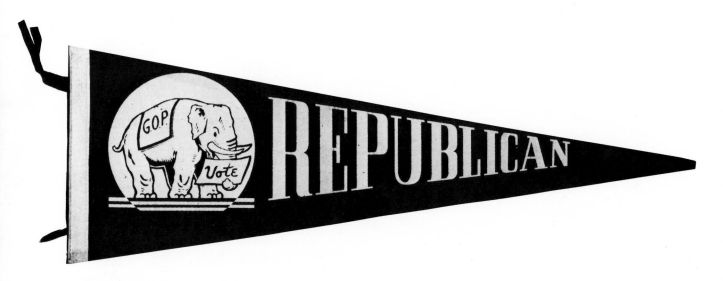

THE ELEPHANT NEVER ELECTED to serve as mascot to the Republican Party but was drafted in 1873 by political cartoonist Thomas Nast. In Nast's drawing (*opposite*) the elephant looks as pleased about his new position as the Democratic donkey.

Little did Nast know what he had started. By 1928 Herbert Hoover had his likeness in the howdah's spot on an elephant bank, and Wendell Willkie appropriated the bumper of an automobile for his message to the voters.

No other Republican contender quite took the elephant to heart as did Dwight Eisenhower. The mascot appeared on badges, on scarves, and even as a miniature doll (resembling more the elephant's legendary nemesis, the mouse). The Thailand government sent the incumbent President Eisenhower a teak state elephant (*opposite*), wishing that "this ancient symbol of Siam be a symbol of the solidity and strength of our friendship," much as America's voters viewed the popular hero of World War II.

In 1948 Dewey had the polls, Truman had the votes—and Henry Wallace had the songs:

The donkey is tired and thin,
The elephant thinks he'll move in,
They yell and they fuss,
But they ain't fooling us,
'cause they're brothers right under the skin.

It's the same, same Merry-go-Round,
Which one will you ride this year?
The donkey and elephant bob up
    and down on
The same Merry-go-Round.

The elephant comes from the North,
The donkey may come from the South,
If you'll look you'll find,
The donkey's behind,
But they got the same bit in their mouth!

If you want to end up safe and sound,
Get offa the Merry-go-Round;
To be a real smarty,
Just join the New Party,
And get your two feet on the ground!

"It's the Same Merry-go-Round," from *Songs for Wallace* © 1948 by Ray Glaser and Bill Wolff

MODERN ARTISANS in countries where the elephants have appeared just in zoos, if at all, are limited only by their imaginations. The small wooden toy opposite is from Denmark, the hanging piñata from Mexico, and the quizzically inquiring elephant from Guatemala.

So oft in theologic wars,
  the disputants, I ween,
Rail on in utter ignorance
  of what the others mean
And prate about an elephant
  Not one of them has seen!

from John Godfrey Saxe's poem,
The Blind Men and the Elephant

IN SPITE OF ITS SIZE, an elephant can fit into almost any surrounding and find a function to perform. The stone carving (*opposite, above*) is at home in a garden and makes a handy, and informal, seat. The leather elephant (*opposite, below*) lives in a den—the human kind—and doubles as a footstool. The demurely smiling elephant replaces a piggy for the collection of coins.

But what is that silly thing doing with its feet over its ears?

....de gracieux éléphants ailés
qui chassent le Malheur
loin de Célesteville,
et ramènent avec eux
le Bonheur .—
A ce moment, il se réveille,
et se sent mieux.